MuscleCarToons

by Jeff Hobrath

JeffHobrath.com

©2020, Jeff Hobrath

ISBN: 9798587050594

Dedicated with love to Melisa and in loving memory of Marion.

ROUTE
66

U.S.A

U.S.A.

USA-1

U.S.A.

Checkout how I create my cartoons from sketch to vector and view my free illustration tutorials at youtube.com/jeffhobrath

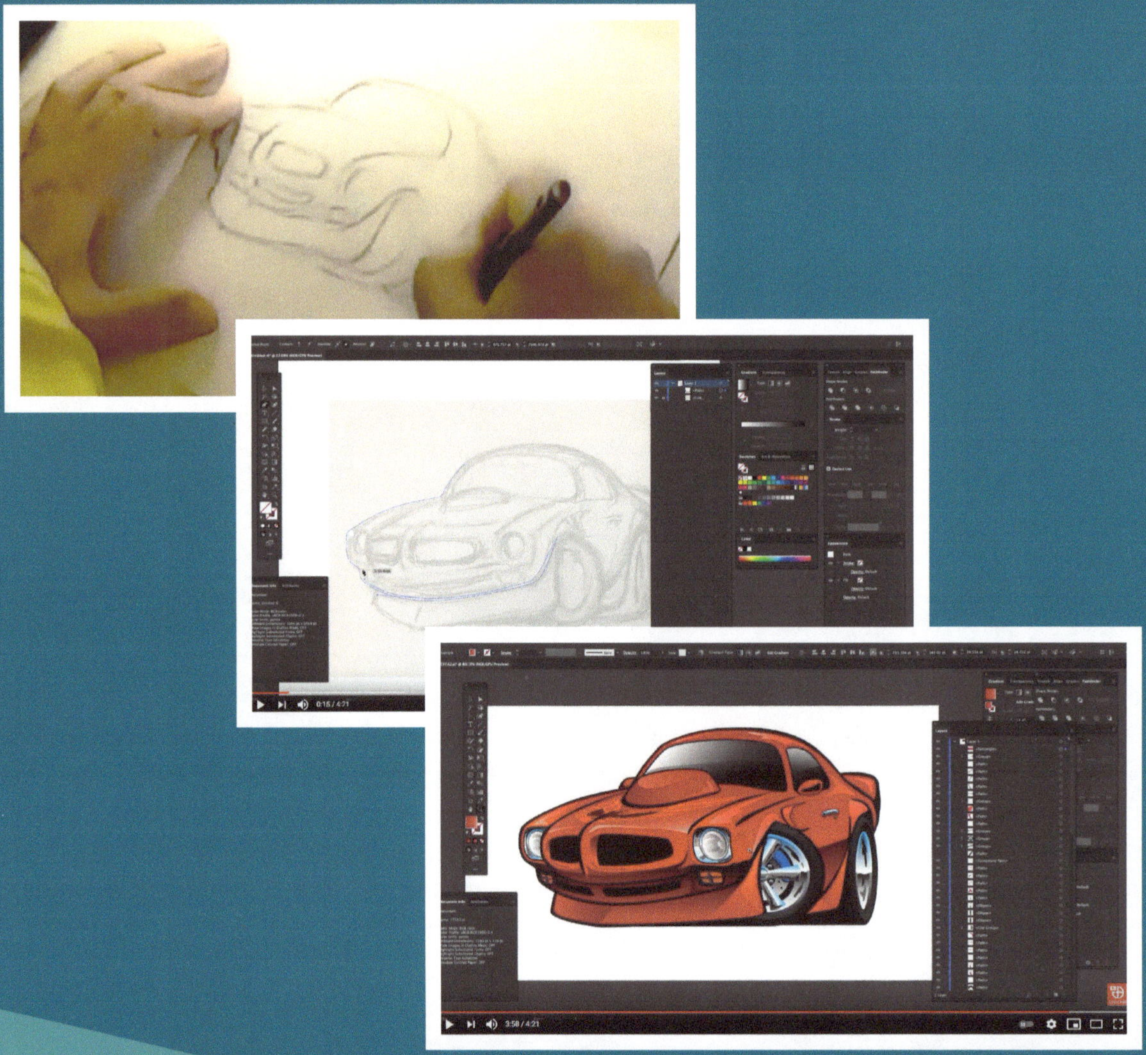

Want some cool MuscleCarToons merch?
Visit MuscleCarToons.com for
T-shirts, posters, stickers and more!